berklee

jazz

piano

Edited by Rajasri Mallikarjuna

RAY SANTIS

Berklee Press

Vice President: David Kusek
Dean of Continuing Education: Debbie Cavalier
Chief Operating Officer: Robert F. Green
Managing Editor: Jonathan Feist
Editor: Rajasri Mallikarjuna
Contributing Editors: Stephany Tiernan, Susan Gedutis-Lindsay
Editorial Assistants: Emily Goldstein, Jonathan Whalen
Additional Proofreading: Masako Yotsugi
Photographer (Cover): Gerald Siddons
Cover Designer: Kathy Kikkert

ISBN 978-0-87639-050-4

1140 Boylston Street
Boston, MA 02215-3693 USA
(617) 747-2146

Visit Berklee Press Online at
www.berkleepress.com

DISTRIBUTED BY

HAL•LEONARD®
CORPORATION
7777 W. BLUEMOUND RD. P.O. BOX 13819
MILWAUKEE, WISCONSIN 53213

Visit Hal Leonard Online at
www.halleonard.com

CONTENTS

CD TRACKS

From Left to Right:
Gene Roma, Drums
Masako Yotsugi, Piano
Ray Santisi, Piano
Greg Loughman, Bass
Recorded at PBS Studios by Peter Kontrimas.

FOREWORD

For fifty years, Ray Santisi has been developing a method for teaching jazz piano. His organic, exciting process involves analyzing and utilizing the harmonic, rhythmic, melodic, and formal vocabulary of jazz theory and applying it directly to the piano.

As his colleague and department chair at Berklee, I have witnessed the transformations of countless pianists through Ray's mentorship. So rapidly, they learn to create exciting and original improvisations, using the techniques Ray puts forth in this book. Many of the world's most celebrated jazz pianists and arrangers have studied with Ray: Keith Jarrett, Diana Krall, and others. His studio has been a music laboratory for exploring the most effective ways to develop the skills necessary to become a great jazz pianist.

Over time, Ray developed a vocabulary to describe some of the activities and processes that he considers necessary to achieve this goal: particalizing, pianisticizing, melodizing, and so many others. These terms describe the critical processes of the jazz language and speaking it through the piano. Many of these have become core pedagogy in the Berklee piano curriculum.

Ray's exercises and concepts are contained in this distinguished volume, which will take you on a unique journey of the jazz piano. They take on lives of their own and open up the infinite creative possibilities of jazz piano improvisation.

Listen carefully to the accompanying recording, and remember that the goal is to allow these exercises to spin into music while you are mastering the techniques. Technique and music should be developing at the same time. That's what will keep you motivated and excited!

Stephany Tiernan, Chair of the Piano Department
Berklee College of Music

PREFACE

This book offers beginning to advanced techniques that will allow you to learn how to fill the many roles that the pianist can take in jazz music. Depending on whether you are playing solo or in an ensemble, your role might be to play a single-line melody, chords, or a bass line, with a wide variety of dynamics, a tremendous range, and with tremendous facility.

The techniques chosen for discussion here are based on the piano curriculum at Berklee College of Music. Each chapter explores a specific technique or techniques with basic explanations and examples, covering required material from all six levels of piano instruction at Berklee. (See appendix C.)

The suggested practice exercises will help make these techniques second nature. Suggested fingerings show how you might best utilize your fingers. Lead sheets (tune charts with melody and chord symbols) and piano arrangements of some of my original tunes will help you to practice applying these concepts (see appendices A and B).

I hope that it brings you tremendous facility and freedom of expression.

—Ray Santisi

CHAPTER 1

Mastering Chords

CHORD TYPES

There are seven basic jazz chords.

Type	Major 6	Minor 6	Minor 7	Minor 7♭5	Dominant 7	Diminished 7	Major 7
Symbol	6	−6	−7	−7♭5	7	°7	Maj7
Formula	1, 3, 5, 6	1, ♭3, 5, 6	1, ♭3, 5, ♭7	1, ♭3, ♭5, ♭7	1, 3, 5, ♭7	1, ♭3, ♭5, ♭♭7	1, 3, 5, Maj7

Fig. 1.1. Chord Types

On piano, these chords are generally played as 4-note voicings in *close position*, meaning that all notes are set within one octave (see figure 1.1). Whether harmonizing a melody or played as a *comping* part (chordal accompaniment), chords are most commonly played as 4-note close voicings.

These chords may appear in different *inversions*—note orders, defined by the voicing's bottom note. Choosing different inversions helps to create harmonic activity without changing chord identity.

- *Root position* means that the chord root is on the bottom.
- *First inversion* means that the third is on the bottom.
- *Second inversion* means that the fifth is on the bottom.
- *Third inversion* means that the sixth or seventh is on the bottom.

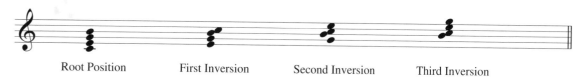

Root Position First Inversion Second Inversion Third Inversion

Fig. 1.2. Inversions

Chord notes may be played simultaneously or sequentially ("broken").

Fig. 1.3. Simultaneous vs. Broken Chords

VOICE LEADING

By *voice leading* chords smoothly—choosing inversions that minimize note movement—your comping will sound more refined and be easier to play. In figure 1.4, note how using the second inversion of E7 allows you to keep two common tones going from B–7♭5 to E7, and one from E7 to B♭7.

Fig. 1.4. Voice Leading

PRACTICE

Learning to play all chords in all inversions is an essential jazz piano skill. The following types of exercises will help you to build muscle memory and enable you to call upon different inversions spontaneously.

Practice these exercises in two ways:

1. Use the circle of fifths, and practice all seven chord types for two roots per day. Proceed through the circle of fifths, practicing two more roots every day. You will cover all permutations of all basic chords every six days.

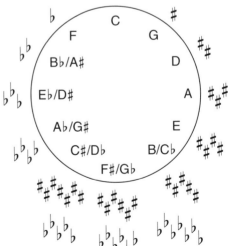

Fig. 1.5. Circle of Fifths

2. Base these exercises on the chords from the new music you are learning, such as the lead sheets in appendix A. Though this doesn't ensure that you'll practice all permutations of all chords, it will directly help you learn your current material.

Examples for the following exercises are based on this lead sheet:

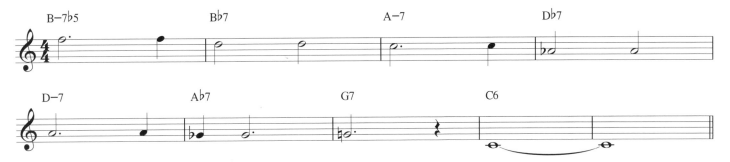

Fig. 1.6. Sample Chord Progression

Exercise 1.1. Inversion Practice: Two Hands Parallel

This essential exercise will help you to build facility playing any chord. Keep your hands one octave apart, and begin with your left hand in the range about two octaves below middle C. Continue it for all chords you are studying, whether in a lead sheet or as you progress through the circle of fifths.

Exercise 1.2. Melodic Chord Tone Units

The right hand plays broken chords (also called *melodizing* the chords) in all inversions. The left hand plays one inversion throughout the entire exercise, and then the next inversion the second time through. Then voice lead the progression. Continue it for all chords you are studying.

TRACK 16

Exercise 1.3. Varied Right-Hand Note Order

This is another version of the Melodic Chord Tone Unit exercise (exercise 1.2), but varies the note order in the right hand. Instead of playing them in the order 1-2-3-4, try instead 1-4-2-3, or a note order of your own choice. Continue it for all chords you are studying. For an added challenge, use smooth voice leading in the left hand.

1-4-2-3

Exercise 1.4. Varied Left-Hand Inversions

This is yet another variation of the Melodic Chord Tone Unit exercise (1.2). Here, in each bar, the left hand plays all the inversions. Continue it for all chords you are studying.

Exercise 1.5. Lead Sheet Practice

To gain a solid command of any lead sheet, use the following practice approach, based on the preceding exercises. You will be playing seventeen choruses of the lead sheet's chord progression, so this is a substantial exercise. Try this on the lead sheets in appendix A.

1. The left hand comps four quarter notes per measure, with a different inversion on each beat. The right hand plays the melody. Play one chorus.
2. The left hand comps the same inversion on each quarter note. The right hand plays 1-2-3-4 broken chords. Play one chorus for each inversion in the left hand.
3. Like (2), but the right hand plays 1-4-2-3 or another pattern.
4. Like (2), but use smooth voice leading in the left hand.
5. Like (2), but use smooth voice leading in the left hand and play the melody with the right hand.

CHAPTER 2

Bass Parts

Jazz pianists often play a bass part in the left hand and melody/chords in the right hand. Bass parts should be simple, favoring the root, octave, and fifth.

Here are three common bass parts, with increased activity in each.

BASS PART 1: Root Only (1)

Fig. 2.1. Bass Parts with Roots

BASS PART 2: Root and Fifth (1-5)

Fig. 2.2. Bass Line with Roots and Fifths

BASS PART 3: Root, Fifth, and Octave (1-8-5-1)

Fig. 2.3. Bass Part with Roots, Fifths, and Octaves

BASS PART 4: Root, Fifth, Octave, and 9 (or ♭9)/3 (1-5-8-9[♭9]/3)

To increase activity, try this variation. Play eighth notes 1-5-8 followed directly with major or minor 7th or augmented 2nd (#9), for more dissonance. With –7♭5, it's 1-5-8-♭3-11.

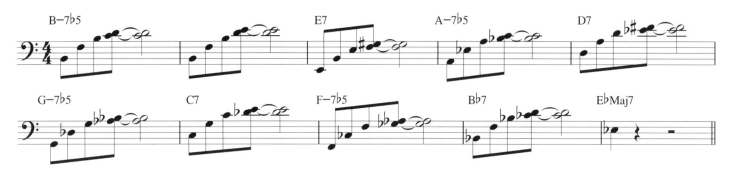

Fig. 2.4. Bass Variation

PRACTICE

Practice the lead sheets in appendix A with a variety of bass lines. Practice different options, to help you determine the level of activity that best suits your desired arrangement.

Exercise 2.1. Root, Fifth, Octave

Practice with the root, fifth, and octave. Play block chords before melodizing the chords (exercise 2.2), as in the example below. The numbers below the staves are suggested fingerings.

TRACK 17

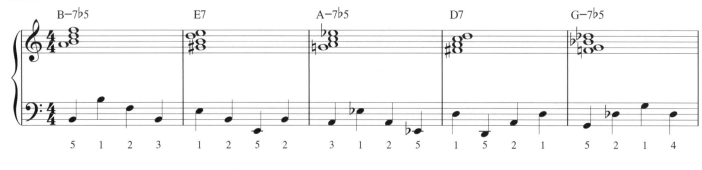

Exercise 2.2. Broken Chords in Right Hand and Root, Fifth, Octave

Practice with the root, fifth, and octave, but melodize the chords, as below.

TRACK 18

Exercise 2.3. Variations

Vary the note order of the root, fifth, and octave in exercise 2.2. For example:
5-1-8-1, 1-8-5-1, 1-5-8-1, 8-1-5-8.

Exercise 2.4. Melody and Bass Line

Play several melodies of your choice with all the different bass line types
presented in this chapter. (Try the lead sheets in appendix A.) Which lines seem most
effective for each melody?

CHAPTER 3

Harmonizing the Melody

Harmonizing a melody means reinforcing it with chords. This provides a bigger, richer sound than the melody alone (also called a "lead line"). Jazz pianists generally harmonize melodies with 4-note chords.

To harmonize a melody, first determine which melody notes are *chord tones* (notes in its associated chord) and which are *non-chord tones* (i.e., notes not in that chord, also called "dissonances"). Most melodies have both chord tones and non-chord tones.

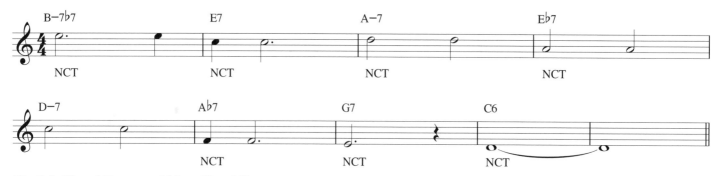

Fig. 3.1. Chord Tones and Non-Chord Tones

Once you know which melody notes are non-chord tones, you can fill in the remaining three chord tones beneath the melody. If the melody note is a chord tone, set the notes directly underneath it. If it is a non-chord tone, omit the first chord tone beneath the melody (giving space to the dissonance), and then fill in the remaining chord tones.

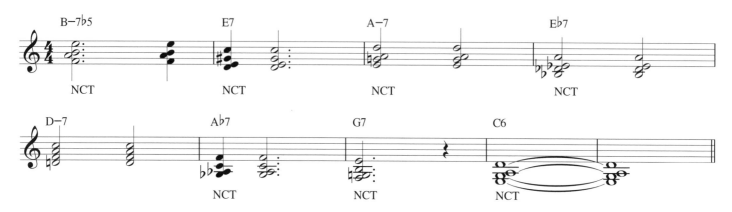

Fig. 3.2. Harmonized Melody

HARMONIZING CHORD TONES VS. NON-CHORD TONES

Harmonize a chord tone as close as possible.

Harmonize a non-chord tone by skipping the chord tone closest to it, so as not to create unwanted dissonance. *This is an essential jazz piano skill.*

Generally, only the most important melody notes are harmonized—notes that occur at the beginnings and ends of phrases or on the strong beats of the harmonic rhythm. Notes of a melody are also important if they are isolated and bear the sound that their chord symbols indicate.

COUPLING NOTES

A *coupling note* is a chord tone used to harmonize a melody note, creating chord fragments. They are used to emphasize important points of the melody. Tensions also can be used as coupling notes (see chapter 4).

TRACK 19

Theme for John

Ray Santisi

Fig. 3.3. "Theme for John" Using Coupling Notes

Notice that fingering has been included in this example. Whichever finger is placed on the melody note will make certain fingers below it available for coupling notes. For example, in the pickup measure in figure 3.3, the 3rd finger is placed on the + of beat 4, allowing fingers 1 and 2 to play coupling notes.

The left hand supports the melody and coupling notes with 4-part closed chords with tension substitutions.

FINGERING FOR COUPLING NOTES

These fingering tips can lead to interesting coupling note options. Refer to exercises 4.4(a), 4.4(b), and 4.4(c) as examples.

1. Use consecutive fingers (1-2-3, 3-4, 4-5, etc.) to play a melody so that other consecutive fingers are available to play coupling notes.

2. The 2nd finger on the melody releases the thumb for coupling activity.
   The 3rd finger on the melody releases the thumb and 2nd finger for coupling activity.
   The 4th finger on the melody releases the thumb, 2nd, and 3rd fingers for coupling activity.
   The 5th finger on the melody releases the thumb, 2nd, 3rd, and 4th fingers for coupling activity.

3. The coupling notes can have either the same or different rhythmic activity as the melody notes they are harmonizing.

4. In the special case of the thumb on the melody note, the 2nd, 3rd, 4th, and 5th fingers are able to play coupling notes above the melody.

5. The thumb can play two coupling notes at the same time; playing minor or major 2nd intervals adds tension to a voicing.

PRACTICE

Exercise 3.1. "Limehouse Blues"

Practice the following harmonization of "Limehouse Blues." Note the different ways that chord tones and non-chord tones are voiced.

Philip Braham/Douglas Furber

Exercise 3.2. Lead-Sheet Practice

Practice these harmonization techniques in the lead sheets in appendix A. Determine which melody notes are most important, decide fingerings for these melodies, and then practice harmonizing them using the methods shown.

Exercise 3.3. Adding Bass Lines

Add bass lines while you play harmonized melodies.

CHAPTER 4

Tension Substitutions

A *tension* is a note that extends a basic chord, such as a 9, 11, or 13. Jazz chords are often developed by using *tension substitutions*—replacing given chord tones with tensions, to offer greater harmonic interest. Each chord type has standard common substitutions that expand the basic chord sound without losing the chord's identity.

BASIC CHORD TYPES AND TENSION SUBSTITUTIONS

Chord Type	Substitution
major 6	9 for 1, sometimes major 7 for 6
minor 6	9 for 1, major 7 for 6
minor 7	9 for 1 only
minor 7♭5	♮11 for ♭3
dominant 7	9, ♭9, or ♯9 for 1
	13, ♭13, or ♭5 for 5
diminished 7	9 for 1, 11 for ♭3, ♭13 for ♭5, Maj7 for 7
major 7	9 for 1

Fig. 4.1. Chord Types and Tension Substitutions

Note that the resulting chords are the same as chords with different names.

Fig. 4.2. Chord Types with Tension Substitutions

PRACTICE

Practice all possible combinations of chords and substitutions. This will open your ears to many voicing possibilities and will give you more flexibility and creativity in your soloing and comping. Use chords from the cycle of fifths or your repertoire.

Exercise 4.1. Basic Comparison

This essential exercise will help you memorize the basic substitutions for all chord types.

Using the chart on the preceding page, adapt this exercise to all chords in any lead sheet(s) from appendix A.

Exercise 4.2. Roots

Roots in the bass intensify the dissonances brought by the tension substitutions.

Exercise 4.3. Melodic Tension Units

Practice the progressions to the lead sheets in appendix A in their standard form and with tension substitutions for each chord. Feel free to use all the chord practice techniques we have been discussing, including different voicings and bass lines.

Exercise 4.4. Harmonizing Melodies

The following melodies have been harmonized as discussed in chapter 3, but with tension substitutions. Practice these tunes, and then apply the same techniques to other tunes.

TRACK 20

(a)

Osco Trane

Ray Santisi

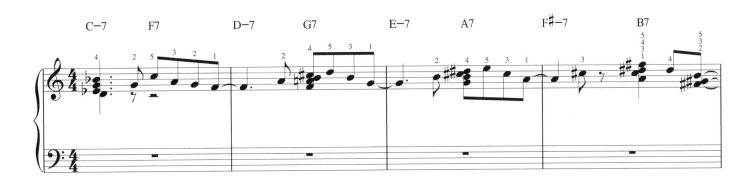

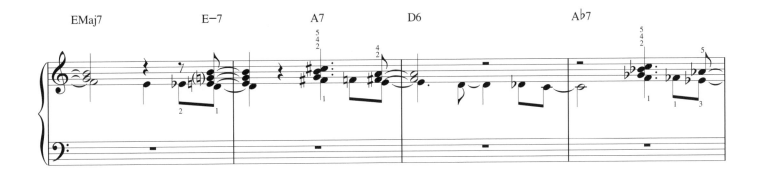

(b)

Theme for John

Ray Santisi

(c)

Paper Doll

Johnny S. Black

Exercise 4.5. "Like, Blues"

TRACK 1

Practice the "Like, Blues" etude in appendix B. This arrangement contains examples of 3-part chords with tensions in the left hand.

CHAPTER 5

Syncopation

A common jazz technique for interpreting melodies is *syncopating* rhythms—playing them off the beat. This can enliven an otherwise static melody.

Here is an example of a melody in its original form.

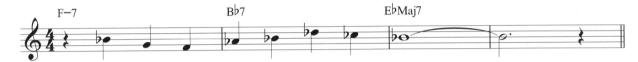

Fig. 5.1. Melody without Syncopation

To add syncopation, first consider the underlying subdivision of the basic pulse. This is also known as the "feel." This example has an eighth-note feel.

Fig. 5.2. Subdivisions

Then move some of the notes that originally occurred *on* the beat instead *off* the beat, either before (anticipating) or after (delaying) the original attack.

Fig. 5.3. Syncopated Rhythm

This yields the following line.

Fig. 5.4. Syncopated Rhythm

PRACTICE

These practice exercises will help you become comfortable incorporating syncopations into your playing. Practice each lead line using the approach in each exercise. Then apply these skills to the tunes in appendix A.

Exercise 5.1. Melody and Bass Line

Practice this syncopated version of the melody to "Avalon" with roots in the bass.

Exercise 5.2. Melody and Active Bass Line

Practice the first four bars of the melody to "Avalon" with a more active bass line
of roots and fifths than in exercise 5.1.

Avalon

Exercise 5.3. Melody, Chords, and Bass

This exercise harmonizes the first four measures of "Avalon" while using roots
and fifths in the bass.

TRACK 21

Avalon

CHAPTER 6

Comping in Rhythm

As we discussed earlier, comping is a form of accompanying or complementing a song's melody or solos. The most standard of the comping methods we have gone through is 4-part close voicings with tension substitutions. These chords are usually played using syncopation.

First consider the underlying subdivision of the basic pulse. This is also known as the "feel." We will consider an eighth-note feel, as we did in chapter 5.

Then play the chords indicated by chord symbols *off* the beat instead of *on* the beat, either before (anticipating) or after (delaying) the original attack.

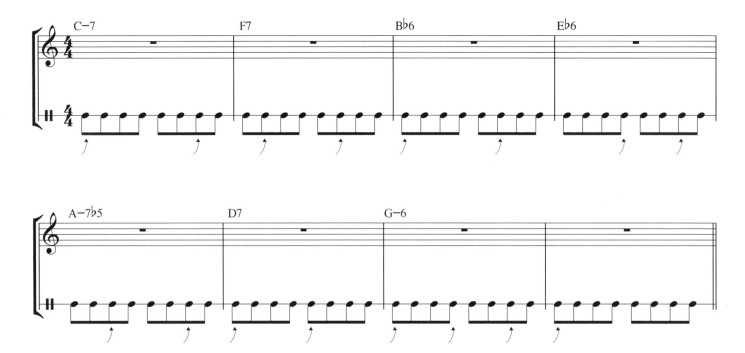

Fig. 6.1. Comping Using Syncopation

"RANDOM" COMPING

Another way to use these voicings are on random attacks on beats while playing a walking bass line.

Random comping is based on syncopation. To get comfortable with random comping, first choose a tempo. Then choose a subdivision, as you did in chapter 5, and place attacks where you feel it best complements the melody. Meanwhile, the left hand can play a walking bass line or additional notes below the right-hand voicing on random attacks independent of when the right hand plays.

Here is an example of random comping using any note of the chord in the left hand part.

Fig. 6.2. Simple Random Comping

Here is another example of random comping. The bass part consists of attacks on downbeats. Notice that chords are not always voice led.

Fig. 6.3. Random Comping with Bass Activity

Here is an example of random comping that has a more active bass line than figure 6.3.

Fig. 6.4. Random Comping with Active Bass Line

PARTICALIZED RANDOM COMPING

Particalization is the use of displaced chord fragments. In random comping, you can particalize a voicing rather than use the entire chord. This can reduce conflicts in register between you and the soloist.

Here is a comping part.

Fig. 6.5. Comping without Rhythm

Here is a particalized random comping part for that same progression.

Fig. 6.6. Particalized Random Comping

Here is the original progression.

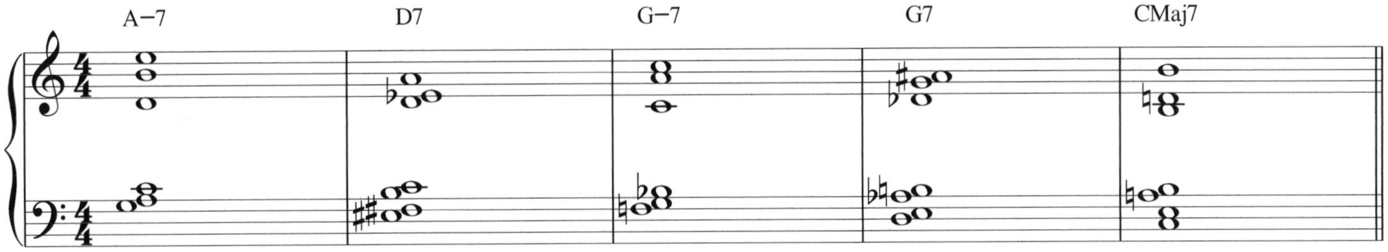

Fig. 6.7. Progression before Particalization

Here is that progression with particalized random comping.

Fig. 6.8. Particalized Random Comping

Here is an example of particalized random comping in "Sapphire," bars 31 and 32.

Fig. 6.9. Particalized Random Comping: Bars 31 and 32 of "Sapphire"

PIANISTICIZING YOUR ACCOMPANIMENT

Pianisticizing a progression adds variety by using multiple registers of the keyboard, displacing the components of the voicings. The melody stays intact.

Here is a pianisticized passage in "Sapphire."

Fig. 6.10. Bars 31 to 34 from "Sapphire" (Pianisticized)

Fig. 6.11. "Sapphire"

In figure 6.12, the melody of "Theme for John" has been harmonized and pianisticized with additional activity in the left hand.

Fig. 6.12. Pianisticizing "Theme for John"

Other pianistization examples on the CD include tracks 2, 5, 8, 11, and 14.

Windows for Pianisticization

When you have a sustained melody note, you can use that space as a *window* to pianisticize it by:

1. Filling it with a simple melody based on the chord scale.
2. Approaching the target chord with V7, subV7, or V7sus4 or a passing diminished chord derived from an incomplete dominant 7th with tension ♭9.
3. Using constant structures.

In this example, the window is closed with a simple connecting line, the last note of which approaches the target melody note in the following measure.

Fig. 6.13. Closed Window with Harmonization

Here is that same window pianisticized.

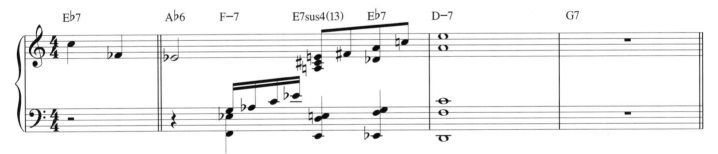

Fig. 6.14. Closed Window Pianisticized

Here is an example of filling in a window played by a soloist. The soloist's note is common to each chord. Note the derivative bass line (see chapter 7).

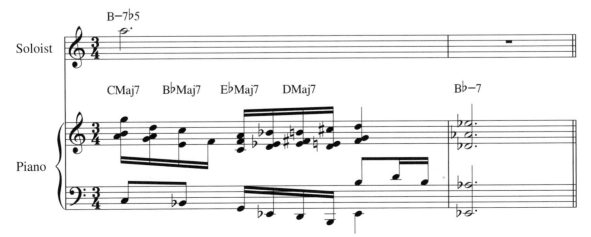

Fig. 6.15. Windows with Constant Structures

PRACTICE

Exercise 6.1. Syncopated Comping

Comp this progression, attacking on the eighth-note subdivisions indicated by
arrows.

Exercise 6.2. Random Comping

Choose any lead sheet from appendix A to practice random comping, playing
right hand voicings on random attacks while the left hand plays a walking bass
line. Then try the same tune with random attacks in both hands, with the left
hand providing additional notes to the right-hand voicing.

CHAPTER 7

Walking Bass Lines

Walking bass lines add forward momentum to your playing. In a walking bass line, the left hand plays a note on every beat (quarter notes, in 4/4). There is an implied triplet feel (like swung eighth notes), often with grace-note skips peppering the basic rhythm. Especially when playing solo piano, without a bass player, a walking bass part can add vital energy and color.

Notes in walking bass lines are of two essential types: target notes and approach notes.

- *Target notes* are chord tones on strong beats (1 and 3, in 4/4). They are landing points, with minimal tension.
- *Approach notes* connect or lead to the target notes. They are points of tension and require resolution to a target note.

To construct a walking bass line, begin by setting the target notes—chord tones (any inversion) on beats 1 and 3.

Fig. 7.1. Target Notes

There are many ways to choose approach notes. Here are three potential sources.

1. The diminished-7 chord based on a root a half step below the current chord's root, called an "approach chord." This dominant sound creates a strong motion towards resolution, when followed by a chord tone. Figure 7.2 shows the target notes for the C–7 chord, based on B°7.

Target Notes: Chord Tones of C–7
Approach Notes: Based on B°7

Fig. 7.2. Approach Chord

Here is a bass line built using this approach. The approach chords are B°7 for the
C–7 and E°7 for the F7.

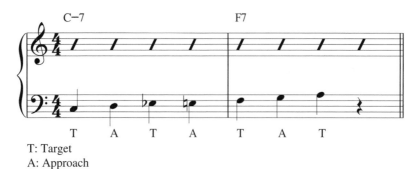

T: Target
A: Approach

Fig. 7.3. Bass Line Using Approach Notes

2. Chromatic approaches from below. This yields a similar line, but in bar
    2, the G approach note (based on E°7) becomes G♯, the chromatic half
    step below A.

Fig. 7.4. Bass Line with Chromatic Approaches

3. Scale tones from above. Choose the scale based on the chord symbol,
    key signature, and the overall harmonic region.

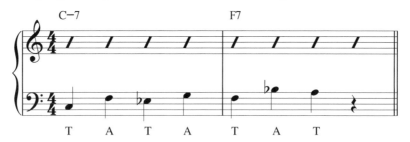

Fig. 7.5. Bass Line with Scale Approach Notes

In practice, you will use a combination of these techniques to create your bass
lines.

Fig. 7.6. Walking Bass Line Using Approaches

HARMONIZATION WITH MAJOR AND MINOR TRIADS

Choose bass notes not found in the triad that result in the desired rate of dissonance. Triads and bass line may be combined with diatonic or non-diatonic triads, and a diatonic or non-diatonic bass line.

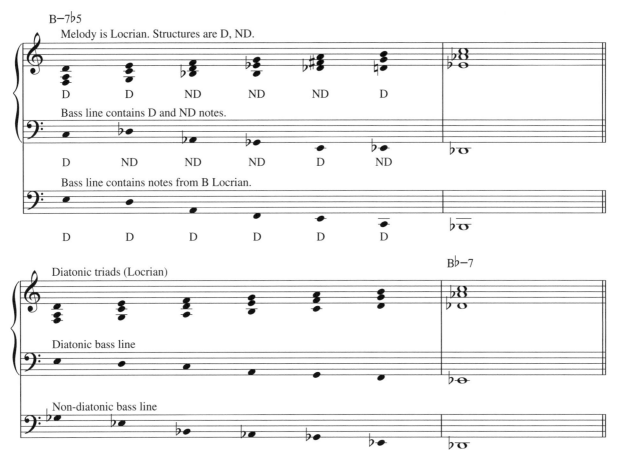

Fig. 7.7. Diatonic and Non-Diatonic Triads and Bass Lines

DERIVATIVE BASS LINES

You can use *derivative bass lines*, or any bass line containing more than just roots, to fill in windows (chapter 6). You can use either diatonic or non-diatonic triads in the right hand. Here are measures 19 to 21 from "Theme for John," harmonized with major triads, choosing a bass note not found in the chord, resulting in the desired level of dissonance.

Fig. 7.8. "Theme for John," Measures 19–21

PRACTICE

Practice these two progressions to get more comfortable with playing walking bass lines. Then create your own walking bass lines to the progressions in appendix B, as well as standards such as "Stella by Starlight," "I Love You," "Autumn in New York," and "Blue Bossa."

Exercise 7.1. Walking Bass Lines

TRACK 23

(a)

(b)

CHAPTER 8

Open Voicings

Open voicings are 4-part chords that are spread larger than a single octave. Jazz pianists frequently use open voicings when harmonizing a tune, comping, and soloing.

DROP VOICINGS

Drop-2

A drop-2 voicing is an open voicing built from a basic 4-part close voicing by dropping the voice that is second from the top down an octave. Use the following steps to make a drop-2 voicing:

Step 1. Start with a basic 4-part close voicing.

Fig. 8.1. Basic Close Voicing

Step 2. Lower the voice that is second from the top, or the first note below the melody note, down an octave. All other voices remain in place.

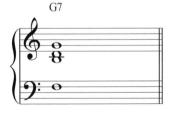

Fig. 8.2. Drop-2 Voicing

Drop-3

A drop-3 voicing is an open voicing built from a basic 4-part close voicing by dropping the third voice from the top down an octave.

Using a drop-3 voicing is not as common as the drop-2 voicing. It works nicely if the root is added to the voicing, especially in the inversion below. (Doubling the root in an inner voice is okay.) The voicing creates a second interval at the top, which sounds weak harmonically. The added root makes the voicing sound stronger.

Step 1. Start with a basic 4-part close voicing.

Fig. 8.3. Basic Close Voicing

Step 2. Lower the voice that is third from the top, or the second note below the melody note, down an octave. All other voices remain in place. Note that the top voice is doubled.

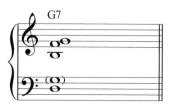

Fig. 8.4. Drop-3 Voicing

Drop-4

A drop-4 voicing is an open voicing built from a 4-part close voicing by dropping the fourth voice from the top down an octave. Like the drop-3 voicing, it is not as common as a drop-2 voicing.

Step 1. Start with a basic 4-part close voicing.

Fig. 8.5. Basic Close Voicing

Step 2. Lower the voice that is fourth from the top, or the third note below the melody note, down an octave. All other voices remain in place.

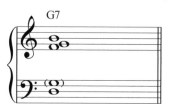

Fig. 8.6. Drop-4 Voicing

Drop-2 and -4 Voicings

Dropping two voices on the same chord is a common technique, the most frequently occurring of these being the drop-2 and -4 voicing. Since the intervals between the notes of this voicing are more equidistant than those of any other voicing, it has the most balanced sound amongst them.

Step 1. Start with a basic 4-part close voicing.

Fig. 8.7. Basic Close Voicing

Step 2. Lower the voices that are second and fourth from the top, or the first and third notes below the melody note, down an octave. All other voices remain in place.

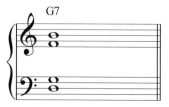

Fig. 8.8. Drop-2 and -4 Voicing

ADDING THE ROOT

On any open voicings, the chord root (or its substitutes: ♭9, 9, ♯9) can be included as an inner voice. Especially the root adds stability to the chord's identity.

SUBSTITUTE TENSIONS

The final step to creating a drop voicing is to substitute tensions where possible.

Here is the drop-2 voicing from above (figure 8.2) with tension 13, E, replacing 5, D. The root is doubled.

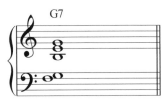

Fig. 8.9. Drop-2 Voicing with Tension 13

In general with open voicings, avoid creating a flat-9th interval between any two voices in the drop-2 voicing, since it results in strong dissonance. The basic rule for avoiding a flat-9th interval is not to combine natural and altered tensions of the same degree, such as ♮13/♭13, ♮9/♯9, ♮5/♭5, or ♮5/♭13. The forbidden ♭9 interval may be neutralized by inverting to a Maj7 interval, thus reducing the sharp dissonance of ♭9. This could be considered to become a transitory matter of personal taste.

Here is the drop-2 and -4 voicing from above (figure 8.8) with tensions 9, ♭13, and 13. The ♭13 and ♮13 create a flat-9th interval that should be avoided.

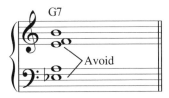

Fig. 8.10. Drop-2 and -4 Voicing with Tensions

Substituting tensions may cause open voicings to sound incomplete. Add the root in any voice to create stability.

Here is the drop-4 voicing from above with substitute tensions 9 for 1 and ♭13 for 5. The root is added to give the chord more stability.

Fig. 8.11. Drop-4 Voicing with Tensions and Added Root

RANGE

Each kind of voicing is typically used in a certain range on the keyboard:

Upper Range   Drop 2 and 4
    (About middle C up to A an octave above)
Middle Range   Drop 2, Drop 3, Drop 4
    (About D below middle C to A above middle C)
Lower Range   Closed
    (Anything lower than D below middle C)

PRACTICE

The following exercises will help you to become comfortable with drop voicings. Use the following approaches with them.

(a) Practice the top line in the right hand. Then play the melody in the right hand and play the harmonizing close chords in the left hand.

(b) Practice the open voicings so that the right hand takes the top voice and the left hand plays the bottom three voices. If the left hand is unable to reach all three, have the right hand play the voice(s) it cannot reach.

Once you have mastered them, apply the techniques used to the lead sheets in appendix A.

Exercise 8.1. "Theme for John"

TRACK 24

Ray Santisi

Drop 2+4

Exercise 8.2. "Ramblas"

Practice the following tune, "Ramblas," in the same manner as explained in exercise 8.1.

Ray Santisi

Exercise 8.3. Tunes with Drop Voicings

In appendix B, "Like, Blues," "Little Sue," "Perry's Parasol," "Take Two," and "Theme for John" all contain drop-2 voicings. Choose a few that you like and practice them.

CHAPTER 9

5-Part Fourth Voicings

The *5-part fourth voicings* are extensions of open voicings, built in fourths. They can be diatonic or non-diatonic.

Diatonic fourth voicings include notes from the scale associated with its key. Starting from the melody note, add notes a fourth below.

For major chords, avoid the 4th and freely substitute the 7th for the root. Here are the inversion possibilities of diatonic 5-part fourth voicings built from notes of the chord scale for CMaj7.

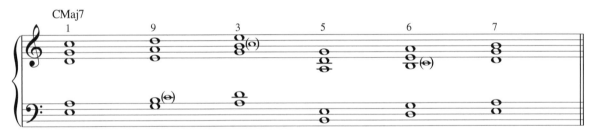

Fig. 9.1. Major Diatonic Fourth Voicings

For minor chords, avoid the 6th degree.

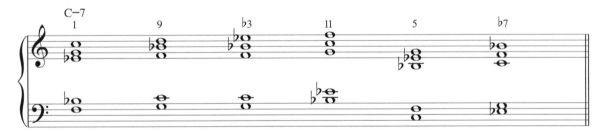

Fig. 9.2. Minor Diatonic Fourth Voicings

Here is an example of harmonizing melody notes using diatonic fourth voicings.

Fig. 9.3. Melody Notes Harmonized by Diatonic Fourths

Non-diatonic fourth voicings occur when the melody note is harmonized using perfect fourths. If the notes move the exact same interval to the next chord, they are also *parallel.* Here is an example of a parallel voicing of perfect fourths.

Fig. 9.4. Perfect/Parallel Non-Diatonic Fourth Voicing

PRACTICE

Exercise 9.1. Diatonic Fourth Voicings

Practice the following voicings of the major and minor chords (figures 9.1 and 9.2) in C. Then practice them in all keys. Use the various chord practice techniques we have been studying.

CMaj7

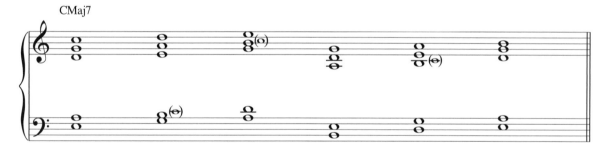

C–7

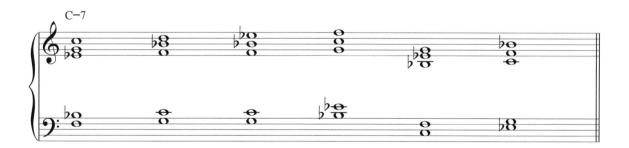

Exercise 9.2. "Perry's Parasol"

Ray Santisi

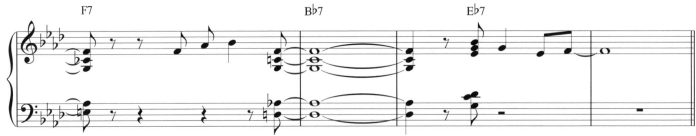

Exercise 9.3. "Take Two"

Practice "Take Two" from appendix B, which is a good example of harmonizing a melody using fourth voicings.

Exercise 9.4. Lead-Sheet Practice

Practice harmonizing melodies using fourth voicings using the lead sheets in appendix A.

CHAPTER 10

Upper-Structure Triads

A triad that contains one or more tensions is called an *upper-structure triad*.

Dominant-7th chords can be voiced using upper-structure triads, in addition to upper-structure fourth voicings.

Upper-structure triads can be played by the right hand. Generally, the left hand plays the tritone (3rd and 7th) of the chord. The right hand plays a triad, avoiding triads that include the chord's 4th or major 7th. You can also overlap the triads and tritones, creating less open voicings. To enhance, replace the third with the fourth, making more triads available (36). The upper-structure triads remain; just avoid the flat-9th interval. (If it occurs, interchange the voices.)

There are 48 possible triads in all (twelve roots times four qualities). Avoiding the 4th and major 7th degrees leaves 26 triads available for C7:

Fig. 10.1. Triads

Here are examples of a dominant-7th chord with upper-structure triads.

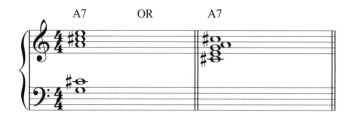

Fig. 10.2. Dominant-7th Chord with No Tension

For diatonic dominant-7th chords, all altered tensions can be used.

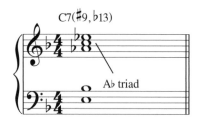

Fig. 10.3. Upper-Structure Triad from Altered Tensions

For non-diatonic dominant-7th chords ♭II7, II7, IV7, ♭VI7, and ♭VII7, choose upper-structure triads that contain ♮9, ♮13, or ♭5. Here is II7 in the key of G major.

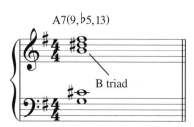

Fig. 10.4. II7 with Upper-Structure Triad

The III7, VI7, and VII7 take upper-structure triads that contain ♭9 or ♭13. Here is III7 in the key of B♭ major.

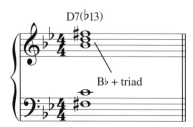

Fig. 10.5. III7 with Upper-Structure Triad

UPPER-STRUCTURE FOURTH VOICINGS

Upper-structure fourth voicings can be used if the root, ♭9, ♮9, ♭5, ♮5, or ♭13 appear in the melody. The left hand plays the chord's tritone (3rd and 7th). The right hand plays chord tones or tensions that create an interval of a fourth. As with upper-structure triads, fourths may overlap. Perfect fourths with the tritone can also be altered. Upper-structure fourths are based (from the bottom up) on the 9-5-1 (perfect fourths), ♯9-♭13-♭9, 3-13-9, ♭13-♭9-♭5, 13-9-5, and ♭7-♯9-♭13. Any low degree may be altered.

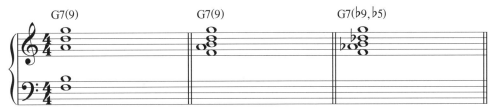

Fig. 10.6. Upper-Structure Fourth Voicing

DOMINANT 7 CONVERTED TO SUS4

Upper-structure triads may be converted into sus4 chords by replacing the left-hand tritone's 3rd with the 4th. To the left hand's interval of the 4 and ♭7, apply all available upper-structure triads. Avoid the major 7th in any triad. The 3rd and sus4 may appear in the same chord if the 3rd is above the 4th. Avoid ♭9 intervals by exchanging the parts. For example, if you have a C diminished triad above the 4 and ♭7 interval, a ♭9 interval will result between the F and G♭, so exchange the parts so that it becomes a major 7th. Some of these result in standard voicings.

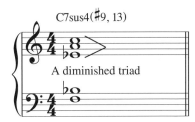

Fig. 10.7. Dominant-7th Chord Converted to Sus4

PRACTICE

Exercise 10.1. Upper-Structure Triad Practice

Choose one possible upper-structure triad for a dominant-7th chord, and practice it in all keys, using cycle 5. For example, play C7 in the left hand with a C minor triad in the right hand, then F7 with an F minor triad, then B♭7 with a B♭ minor triad, etc.

Exercise 10.2. Voice-Leading Upper-Structure Triads

TRACK 26

Play the left hand dominant-7th chords through cycle 5 starting on any key. Voice lead in the right hand, and try using the same triad from one chord to the next. For example, in cycle 5, the C minor triad would work on C7 and the next chord, F7.

CHAPTER 11

Larger Voicings

Using 5-, 6-, 7-, and 8-part voicings is an advanced approach to comping, but these voicings generate a rich, full sound and can be used in "random" comping as well. These voicings will inadvertently produce upper-structure triads and upper-structure fourths. As with all other voicing techniques, these give the impression of a somewhat restrictive order of voices. The ultimate goal with all voicing techniques is to create freedom of movement over the keyboard by reshaping or particalizing and pianisticizing (see chapter 6) the strict order.

CREATING LARGER VOICINGS

To create these larger voicings, follow these guidelines:

1. The left hand plays any inversion of chord tones 1, 3, and 7 (i.e., the chord without the 5th).

Fig. 11.1. 1-3-7 Inversion

2. The right hand plays the melody.

Fig. 11.2. Melody in Right Hand

3. Add tensions below the melody.

Fig. 11.3. Tensions

When creating larger voicings, here are some things to avoid:

1. Avoid the 5th unless it is in the melody.

Fig. 11.4. 5th in Melody

2. Avoid doubling a note unless it is in the melody.

Fig. 11.5. Doubling Chord Tones

3. Avoid combining natural and altered functions of the same tension. If a ♭9 interval results between any two voices, then invert to a major-7th interval, thus reducing the rate of dissonance. For example, do not play ♭5 with 5, ♭9 with ♮9, ♯9 with ♮9, or ♭13 with ♮13.

Fig. 11.6. Combining Tensions

4. Avoid the flat-9th interval.

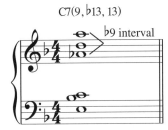

Fig. 11.7. Avoid the Flat-9th Interval

If you have a dominant-7th chord with a sus4, make sure the 3rd is above the sus4 to avoid a flat-9th interval. You can switch the voices of any flat-9th interval to create the less dissonant major 7th interval.

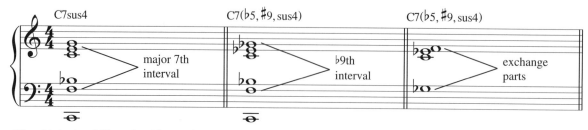

Fig. 11.8. Avoiding the Flat-9th Interval on a Dominant-7th sus4 Chord

Here is an example of a voice-led progression of 6-part voicings.

Fig. 11.9. Voice-Led Progression

PRACTICE

Exercise 11.1. 5- and 6-Part Voicings

Practice the following tune, which you can find in appendices A and B, to get a feel for 5- and 6-part voicings.

Perry's Parasol

Ray Santisi

TRACK 27

Exercise 11.2. Applying Larger Voicings

Use 5-, 6-, 7-, and 8-part voicings on other tunes in appendix A.

CHAPTER 12

Approach-Note Harmonization

To enhance a chord progression, any chord of that progression can be approached by an additional chord. There are five types of "approach" chords: diminished, altered dominant, chromatic, stepwise diatonic, and parallel.

DIMINISHED APPROACH CHORD

Diminished approach chords are diminished chords based on a root a half step below the target chord root. They can approach any type of chord.

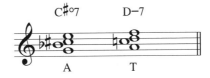

Fig. 12.1. Diminished Approach (A = Approach Chord, T = Target Chord)

In the following excerpt from "Limehouse Blues," the diminished approach is used to approach the D♭9. Though G isn't a half step below D♭, the tension 9 of the D♭9 chord converts the chord to A♭6 and F–7♭5. Therefore, G°7 works since its root is a half step below A♭.

Fig. 12.2. "Limehouse Blues"

ALTERED DOMINANT APPROACH CHORD

Altered dominant approach chords are the altered dominant-7th chords (dominant-7th chords with altered tensions) of their target chord. They are especially effective when the melody moves from 13 to 5, 5 to 13, 5 to ♭13, or ♭13 to ♭5.

Here, an altered V7/V approaches V (key of F) while the melody moves in various ways.

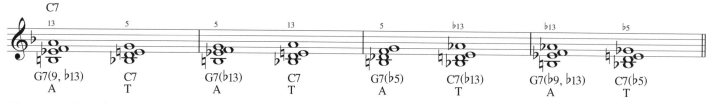

Fig. 12.3. Altered Dominant Approach

Here, the melody moves from 5 to 13 on B♭7. C♭7, the substitute dominant of B♭7, is used to approach B♭7. It contains tensions 9 and ♭5.

Fig. 12.4. Melody Notes 5 to 13

TRACK 28

In the second measure below, F7(♭9) approaches B♭–7.

Fig. 12.5. Applied Altered Dominant Approach

CHROMATIC APPROACH

Chromatic approach chords are based on a root a half step away from any chord tone (or tension) of the target chord.

Fig. 12.6. Chromatic Approach

TRACK 29

This type of approach chord is most useful when the melody moves chromatically.

Fig. 12.7 Applied Chromatic Approach

STEPWISE DIATONIC APPROACH

Stepwise diatonic approach chords belong to the key of the progression. Use them to harmonize a melody moving by step.

If the target is a tonic chord, the approach chord should have a subdominant function. If the target is a subdominant chord, the approach chord should have a tonic function.

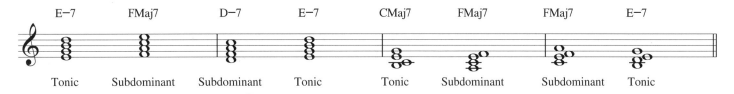

Fig. 12.8. Stepwise Diatonic Approach

In a stepwise diatonic approach, only use a dominant chord as the approach chord if you alter it into a sus4 chord.

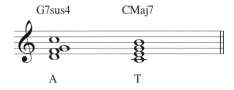

Fig. 12.9. Dominant-7 Sus4 Chord Approaches Tonic

TRACK 30

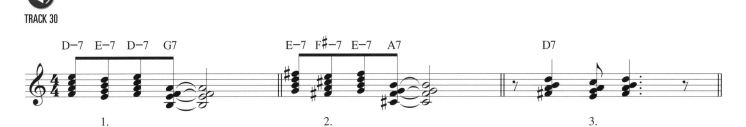

Fig. 12.10. Applied Stepwise Diatonic Approach

PARALLEL APPROACH

Parallel approach chords occur when all the voices of an approach chord move the same interval to the target. Below, all voices in beat 2 move by parallel approach the same interval—one half step—to B♭7 (beat 3). It is thus also a chromatic approach.

Fig. 12.11. Parallel Approach

The first measure of the following excerpt from "Limehouse Blues" displays an example of the parallel approach method. Each note of the A♭Maj7 chord is moving up the same amount, one whole step, to the B♭–7 chord; each note of C–7 moves up one whole step to the A♭6 chord.

TRACK 31

Fig. 12.12. Applied Parallel Approach

PRACTICE

Exercise 12.1. Applied Approach-Note Harmonization

Apply all the approach-note harmonizing methods to the lead sheets in appendix A. "Theme for John" is particularly a good model for approach-note harmonization.

Exercise 12.2. Applied Diatonic Approach

Practice the arranged version of "Sapphire" in appendix B. It contains a good model of the diatonic approach method.

CHAPTER 13

Introduction to Improvisation

To communicate to listeners the chord progression used during an improvisa-tion, jazz pianists can do two things: play chord tones in strict or varying patterns, or play the chord tones that determine the chord's identity on the strong beats of the progression's harmonic rhythm.

The resulting series of notes are called "lines." You can create basic lines using only chord tones, or embellish the lines using additional notes, such as tensions and approach notes. Many of these techniques will be discussed in this chapter.

BASIC MELODIC LINES

To begin improvising, you can use several standard techniques that have already been discussed:

TRACK 32

- Playing chord tones in any order will create a melodic line. (See the "Melodic Chord Tone Units Exercise" in chapter 1.)

Fig. 13.1. Chord Tones

- *Guide tones* (the 3rd and 7th degrees of a chord) give the chord its distinctive quality. Using guide tones in your melody strongly communi-cates the harmonic progression.

Fig. 13.2. Guide Tones

- Playing broken chords with tensions is an easy way to improvise over a progression. (See the "Melodic Tension Units exercise 4.3.)

Fig. 13.3. Broken Chords with Tensions

CARRIER CHORDS

Carrier chords are broken chords with tensions that move to a target note (3rd, root, or fifth). Play only the first note of the melody in each measure, and then play the chord indicated by the chord symbol at that beat as a broken chord with tensions, as in figure 13.4.

a.   Given Melody

b.   Melody with Carrier Chords

TRACK 33

Fig. 13.4. Carrier Chords

APPROACH NOTES

Approach notes added to a melodic line can give that line a more interesting sound, as they did in bass lines (chapter 7) and approach chords (chapter 12). Chord tones can be approached from below or above, either by a diatonic scale step (including tensions) or chromatically. Use scale steps or chromatic approaches in any order and combination to give your lines variety. Approaching chromatically from below only creates a scale-like melodic line, which can be desirable.

The following melody uses chromatic approach notes from below and scale notes from above.

TRACK 34

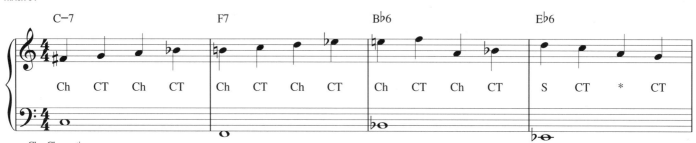

Ch: Chromatic
CT: Chord Tone
 S: Scale Note

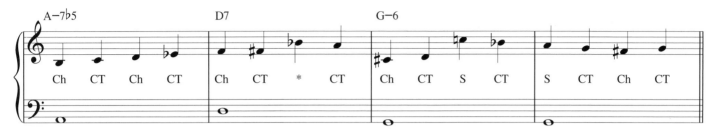

* N.B. For major chords, you can approach 5 with flat 6.

Fig. 13.5. Melody with Chromatic Approaches

In figure 13.6, the top staff is the original melody, and the second staff shows that melody embellished using tension resolution (or chord scale-step approaches down) and chromatic approaches up.

TRACK 35

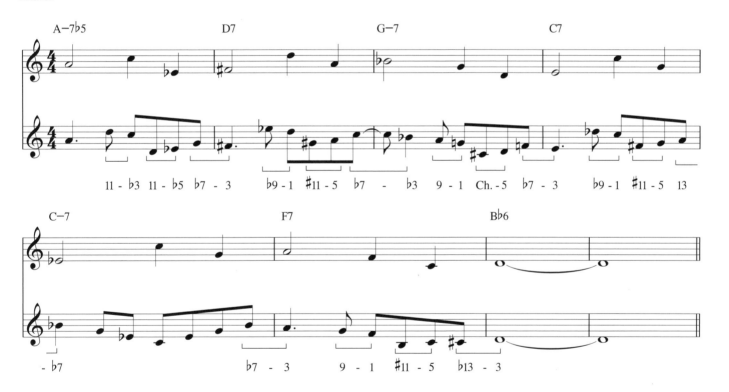

Fig. 13.6. Melody with Tension Resolution

DELAYED RESOLUTION

Delayed resolution is a technique of playing neighbor tones before resolving to a chord tone. Upper and lower neighbor tones are the scale notes that directly follow or precede the chord tone, respectively.

For variety, you can also include the chromatic between the neighbor tone and the resolving note. Usually, these auxiliary notes occur on weak beats. The figure below illustrates delayed resolution.

TRACK 36

T = Target Note

Fig. 13.7. Delayed Resolution Chart

Below, see how delayed resolution can enhance a melody. The top line shows the chord tones that are embellished using delayed resolution in the bottom line.

TRACK 37

Fig. 13.8. Melody with Delayed Resolution

PRACTICE

These exercises will help you to become more familiar with the above improvisation techniques. Then improvise on your own to the progressions from the lead sheets in appendix A.

Exercise 13.1. Approach Note Practice

TRACK 38

Exercise 13.2. Delayed Resolution Practice

Practice the given patterns for each chord quality in the delayed resolution chart up and down the keyboard. Try them in any key, and then vary the note order, just as you did with the Melodic Chord Tone Units (1.2) and Melodic Tension Units (4.3) exercises.

Exercise 13.3. Delayed Resolution Study

Exercise 13.4. Broken Chords with Tensions

In this exercise, the tensions appearing in each broken chord are indicated in the chord symbol. Also, the left hand is playing the same chords in close position.

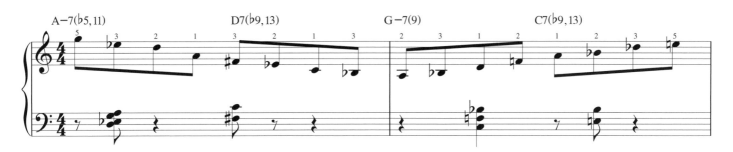

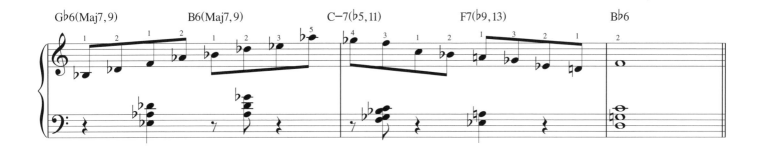

CHAPTER 14

Rhythmic Displacement

Rhythmic displacement is an improvisation technique in which a motif is played by a rhythmic unit (an eighth note, quarter note, sixteenth note, etc.) earlier or later. By shifting the beginning of a phrase from a weak beat to a strong beat or a strong beat to a weak beat, a phrase can be given a fresh new sound.

Below, the motif in the given top line is displaced in four ways: an eighth note later, an eighth note earlier, a quarter note later, and a quarter note earlier.

TRACK 39

Fig. 14.1. Rhythmic Displacement

Rhythmic displacement can be applied to any type of motif. Here is an example of a melodic line with delayed resolution displaced an eighth note later.

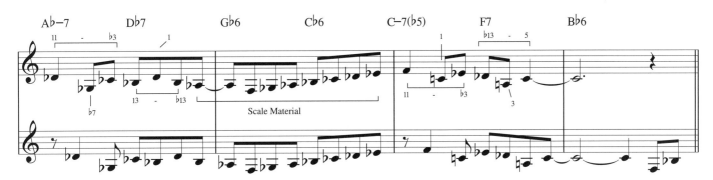

Fig. 14.2. Tension Resolution and Displacement

Grasping rhythmic displacement takes some practice. Practice by shifting motifs or scales to different beats in a measure to get comfortable with this technique. For example, start on beat 1, then start on 1+, then start on 2, etc. It can be easier to plan a rhythm that you will play, as in the following example.

Fig. 14.3. Planned Rhythmic Displacement

SKIPPING NOTES

Another easy method to rhythmic displacement involves skipping notes, or replacing notes with rests. This technique is effective when playing arpeggios, like broken chords with tensions.

Here is the first melody from figure 14.1, and then a version of it with skipped notes.

Fig. 14.4. Melody from Figure 14.1

PRACTICE

Practice these exercises, and then apply the techniques used to your own improvisations of the lead sheets in appendix A.

Exercise 14.1. Rhythmic Displacement

This exercise provides two rhythmically displaced versions of exercise 13.4. Exercise 14.1(a) is an example of skips, and exercise 14.1(b) has been displaced using various rhythmic units.

(a)

(b)

Exercise 14.2. All Techniques Combined

This exercise combines all techniques discussed.

TRACK 40

Exercise 14.3. Application

Add rhythmic displacement to the melodies in appendix B. Then listen to the full band tracks, and focus on the melody. What rhythmic displacement techniques can you identify? Generally, the first time each melody is played, it is fairly true to the written lead sheet. The second time features more rhythmic displacement of the written melodies.

CHAPTER 15

Pentatonic Scales and Chords

Another source of pitches, besides chords tones, is pentatonic scales. A *pentatonic scale* is a five-note scale derived from the major scale. Jazz pianists commonly use the unique sound of pentatonic scales when improvising and comping.

SCALES

The pentatonic scale omits two degrees from the original major scale: the 4th and 7th scale degrees. The major scale's tritone is thus avoided, preventing the feeling that the music needs to resolve. This makes the pentatonic scale ideal for improvisation.

Major Pentatonic

The pentatonic scales available in a major chord begin on its related scale's 1st and 5th scale degrees. In the key of C major, or on a C major chord, the available pentatonic scales for improvising are C pentatonic and G pentatonic.

Fig. 15.1. C Pentatonic Scale

Fig. 15.2. G Pentatonic Scale

Minor Pentatonic

The available pentatonic scales of a minor chord are the pentatonic scales based on its related scale's ♭3rd and ♭7th degrees. In the key of C minor, or on a C minor chord, the available pentatonic scales for improvising are E♭ pentatonic and B♭ pentatonic.

Fig. 15.3. E♭ Pentatonic Scale

Fig. 15.4. B♭ Pentatonic Scale

IMPROVISING WITH PENTATONIC SCALES

A common way to improvise using pentatonic scales is to play them in varying patterns and rhythms up and down the keyboard, as we did with chord tones. Refer to exercises 15.2, 15.3, 15.5, and 15.6 to practice this technique.

Intervallic Links

A contemporary improvisation practice is to link intervals using whole or half steps. These intervals can be major thirds, minor thirds, and perfect fourths, ascending or descending with a half-step link from above or below, constant or variable (shifting direction). Like pentatonic scales, the tritone is omitted, thus negating tonal direction (no cadential material).

Fig. 15.5. All Intervallic Links

You can also alternate pentatonic scales in your improvisations with intervallic links.

Fig. 15.6. Pentatonics and Intervallic Links

Dominant Chord Replacement

Another easy way to improvise with pentatonic scales involves removing the dominant functioning chords from a progression. The tritone is therefore avoided in both the improvisation and the comping. Unlike the tension resolution or melodic tension units methods, it also removes the need to pay attention to chord tones. The result is a contemporary jazz sound.

Let's try it. Here is a simple ii-V-I progression.

Fig. 15.7. ii-V-I Progression

1. Replace all dominant chords with major or minor seventh chords. Use a chord with flat notes to replace a chord with sharp notes, and vice versa. Here, the B♭7 has been replaced with B–7.

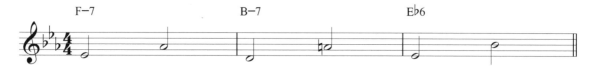

Fig. 15.8. B–7 Replaces B♭7

2. Now use the available pentatonic scales (whose roots are the notes above) to improvise over the progression. In figure 15.8, measures 1 and 2, the pentatonic scales beginning on the flat-3rd degree of each chord are used; the pentatonic scale based on the root is used in measure 3. This improvisation can also be considered as built from inversions of 3-part fourth voicings.

Fig. 15.9. Pentatonic Scales Applied to Progression

Here is another example.

Original Progression:

Fig. 15.10. Progression with Chord Tones

Progression with Replaced Dominant-7 Chord:

Fig. 15.11. Improvisation

THREE-PART FOURTH VOICINGS

While improvising using pentatonic scales on major and minor seventh chords, three-part fourth voicings can be used for comping. These voicings are built with two perfect fourths and are constructed on different degrees of the major and minor chord scales.

They can also be arpeggiated and used to improvise. See practice exercises 15.1 and 15.4.

Three-part fourth voicings for a major chord are constructed on the 2nd, 3rd, 6th, and 7th degrees of the major chord scale.

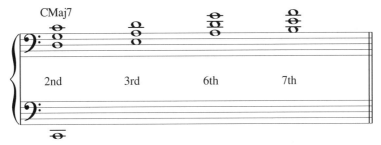

Fig. 15.12. Three-Part Fourth Voicings of CMaj7

Three-part fourth voicings of a minor chord are constructed on the 1st, 2nd, 4th, and 5th degrees of the minor chord scale.

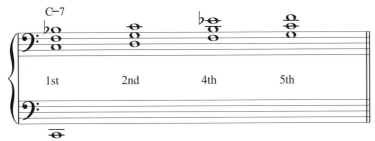

Fig. 15.13. Three-Part Fourth Voicings of C–7

Play chords in both hands, either the same or different, to create rich 6-part voicings when comping.

6/9 Chords and Inversions

The 6/9 chords are major 6 chords with tension 9 substituting the root. The chord tones are consequently 9, 3, 5, and 6. In other words, they contain the notes of the pentatonic scale without the root.

Here is a 6/9 chord and its inversions.

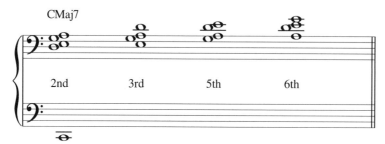

Fig. 15.14. 6/9 Chord and Inversions

6/9 Chord Substitutions

You can also use 6/9 chords to substitute major 6, minor 6, major 7, and minor 7 chords.

If you have a minor-7 chord, you can use a 6/9 chord based on the minor 3rd above or the major 3rd below the minor-7 chord's root. For example, you can substitute a D–7 with F 6/9 or B♭ 6/9. This results in a minor-7 chord without the 3rd. (However, the 6/9 chord found a major 3rd below the root does contain the 3rd.)

An F6/9 substitution would form a voicing made of D–7 chord tones 1, ♭7, 5, and 11. The ♭3 has been omitted. A B♭6/9 substitution would include the ♭3, creating a voicing made of D–7 chord tones 11, ♭3, 1, and ♭7.

USING 6/9 VOICINGS

The 6/9 voicing automatically reduces the resulting flat-9th interval between major 7ths and roots, minor 3rd and 9th, and ♭7 and 13.

PRACTICE

Once you have practiced the following exercises, apply the techniques in this chapter to your improvisations of the lead sheets in appendix B.

Practice the first six exercises the same manner as the Melodic Chord Tone Units exercise. Once you are comfortable playing them, practice the exercises in all other keys. Play the right hand all the way up the keyboard, then down.

Exercise 15.1. Major 3-Part Fourth Voicing Inversions

TRACK 41

Exercise 15.2. Major Pentatonics Starting on the 1st Degree

TRACK 42

Exercise 15.3. Major Pentatonics Starting on the 5th Degree

TRACK 43

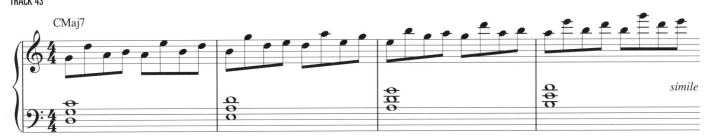

Exercise 15.4. Minor 3-Part Fourth Voicing Inversions

TRACK 44

Exercise 15.5. Minor Pentatonics Starting on the ♭3rd Degree

TRACK 45

Exercise 15.6. Minor Pentatonics Starting on the ♭7th Degree

TRACK 46

Exercise 15.7. Improvising on Replaced Dominant-7 Chords

The top line of chords displays the original version of the progression, and the bottom line is the new contrasting progression without dominant chords, alternating flat regions with sharp regions. The contrasting chord can be found one half step above or below the chord being approached.

TRACK 47

Exercise 15.8. Improvising on Replaced Dominant-7 Chords

TRACK 48

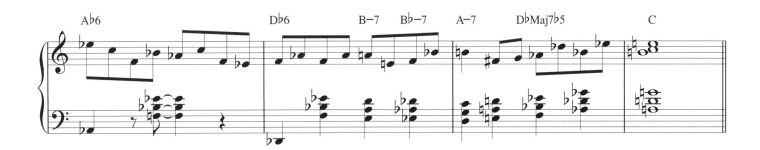

Exercise 15.9. 6/9 Chord Arpeggios with Fourth Voicings

Exercise 15.10. 6/9 Chords with Inversions

Exercise 15.11. Pentatonics Starting on the Root with 6/9 Chords

Exercise 15.12. Pentatonics Starting on the 5th with 6/9 Chords

Exercise 15.13. Improvisation on 6/9 Chord and Inversions

Exercise 15.14. Using 6/9 Chords

1. Analyze these progressions, made up of V/I, V/II, and ♭II7 (substitute dominant).
2. Harmonize melodies using 4-part close voicings, substituting tensions where possible, and using alternate harmonizations.
3. Improve root motion (when the root repeats) by using 11 for 1 with minor-7th chords and ♭5 for 5 in dominant-7th chords.

Exercise 15.15. Intervallic Links

Identify the different types of intervallic links in this exercise. Then improvise on the lead sheets in appendix A using intervallic links in your improvised lines.

CHAPTER 16

Modal Melody and Harmony

MODES

A *mode* is a scale that contains a characteristic pitch that distinguishes it from the major or minor scale from which it is derived.

The major scale is also called the Ionian mode.

Fig. 16.1. Ionian Mode

The Lydian mode is the major scale with a raised 4th degree.

Fig. 16.2. Lydian Mode

The Mixolydian mode is the major scale with a lowered 7th degree.

Fig. 16.3. Mixolydian Mode

The natural minor scale is also called the Aeolian mode.

Fig. 16.4. Aeolian Mode

The Dorian mode is the natural minor scale with a raised 6th degree.

Fig. 16.5. Dorian Mode

The Phrygian mode is the natural minor scale with a lowered 2nd degree.

C Phrygian

Fig. 16.6. Phrygian Mode

The Locrian mode is the natural minor scale with a lowered 2nd and 5th degree.

C Locrian

Fig. 16.7. Locrian Mode

CREATING A MODAL MELODY

A mode, like any other scale, can be the basic structure from which melodies and harmonic frameworks are developed.

When creating a modal melody, follow these conditions:

1. Emphasize the tonic note of the mode. The duration of this note should be longer than the duration of other scale degrees, and it should occur more frequently.
2. Place secondary emphasis on the characteristic pitch of the mode.
3. Melodic cadence, or resolution between degrees 2 and 1 or 7 and 1, is significant.
4. All notes of the mode should be used in the melody. This will eliminate modal ambiguity.

Here is a melody in D Phrygian:

TRACK 49

T: Tonic note
C: Characteristic pitch

Fig. 16.8. Modal Melody

Notice in figure 16.8 that the tonic note, D, occurs more than any other note in this melody, and on most downbeats. The characteristic note of D Phrygian, E♭, occurs twice. Melodic cadences occur at measures 1 to 2 (degrees 7 and 1) and 2 to 3 (degrees ♭2 and 1). All the notes of the D Phrygian scale (D, E♭, F, G, A, B♭, and C) occur at least once.

CREATING A MODAL HARMONIC FRAMEWORK

There are two ways to construct modal harmonic frameworks:

1. Construct a logical bass line by:
   a. Creating a cadence (2 to 1 or 7 to 1) after every three or four notes.
   b. Frequently using chords that contain the mode's characteristic note.
   c. Avoiding the tritone of the tonic scale from which the mode is derived unless you are using the Lydian mode or the Phrygian I chord.
   d. Using chromatic alteration sparingly.

The resulting harmonic frameworks will contain standard chords, and it therefore will sound stable.

Here is a harmonic framework in G Dorian. Notice that a cadence from 7 to 1 occurs between measures 4 and 5, and a cadence from 2 to 1 occurs between measures 7 and 8. Also, chords containing E—the characteristic note of G Dorian—are frequent.

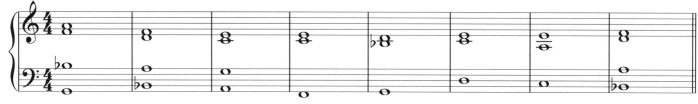

Fig. 16.9. G Dorian Framework

2. Construct the soprano and bass line using contrary motion between them. Roots of standard chords don't necessarily have to be in the bass. The resulting structures will be clusters and voicings in fourths.

Here is an example of a harmonic framework in C Lydian.

Fig. 16.10. C Lydian Framework

ACTIVATED MODAL FRAMEWORKS

TRACK 50

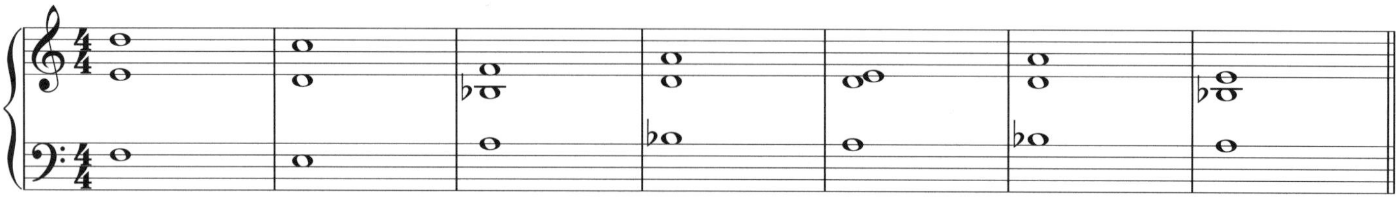

Fig. 16.11. A Phrygian Framework

Fig. 16.12. Activated A Phrygian Framework

COMBINATIONS OF MODES IN MELODY AND HARMONY

When composing modal melodies and harmonic frameworks, you can use more than one mode derived from the same or different key. Here are some examples:

Two Modes from the Same Key Center (G Aeolian over D Phrygian):

Fig. 16.13. G Aeolian Melody over G Phrygian Framework

Two Modes from Different Key Centers (E Phrygian over G Dorian):

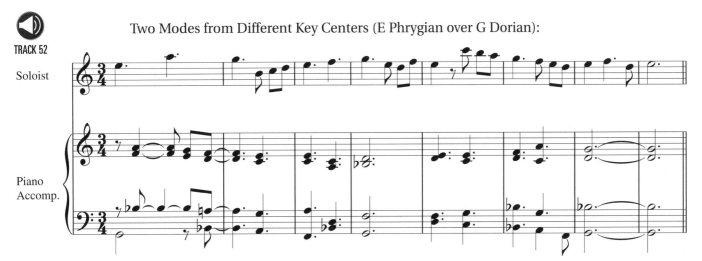

Fig. 16.14. E Phrygian over G Dorian Framework

USING MODES IN IMPROVISATION

You can improvise with modes over any chord type. Make the root of the chord the mode's tonic note. (See figure 16.15.)

Fig. 16.5. Modal Improvisation

PRACTICE

Exercise 16.1. Modal Melodies

Create pure modal melodies in each mode. Vary the time signatures, tempo, dynamic marks, and phrasing. Then use a combination of modes.

Exercise 16.2. Modal Frameworks

Create harmonic frameworks in each mode. Vary time signatures and tempo. Then use a combination of modes.

Exercise 16.3. Pure Modal Melody and Harmony

Create a modal melody and accompaniment in pure modal form.

Exercise 16.4. Modal Melody and Accompaniment

Create a modal melody and accompaniment using a combination of modes.

Exercise 16.5. Modal Improvisation

Improvise on the lead sheets in appendix A. Use the roots of chords to choose which modes you will improvise with.

CHAPTER 17

Jazz Counterpoint

Counterpoint involves one note played against another. The notes are harmonically complementary. Incorporating counterpoint into your soloing involves meticulous work, but it can add a layer of depth to your arrangements.

TENSION RESOLUTION AS COUNTERPOINT

In the rules of jazz counterpoint, tensions on chords must resolve to certain scale degrees.

Downward Resolution

Chord	
Major 6	9-1, Maj7-6, 11-3, ♭6-5
Minor 6	9-1, Maj7-6, 11-♭3, ♭6-5
Minor 7	9-1, 11-3, ♭6-5
Minor 7(♭5)	9-1, 11-3, ♭13-♭5
Dominant 7	9-1, ♭9-1, 11-3, ♭5-3, 13-5, ♭13-5
	Tension to Tension Resolution:
	9-♭9, ♯9-♭9, 13-♭13, ♭13-♭5, ♭13-5, 13-♭13-♯11-5
Diminished 7	Tensions a whole step above a chord tone resolve down to chord tones by step
Major 7	9-1, 11-3, ♭6-5

Fig. 17.1. Tension Resolutions

If a note in either the original melody or contrapuntal melody is a tension, it will represent the chord tone it resolves to.

UPWARD RESOLUTION

Any basic chord tone is resolved to when it is approached chromatically from below.

FOUR-PART COUNTERPOINT

In jazz, you would take the melody and create contrapuntal lines to it using these techniques:

  a. Use stepwise motion. (Avoid using a tension resolution pattern if tension resolution occurs in the original melody.)

Fig. 17.2. Incorrect Tension Resolution

  b. If you use a tension in your contrapuntal melody, it should be of shorter or equal duration to its resolving note.

For example, the ♭9 tension on the third beat of measure 2 in figure 17.2, which lasts for only two beats, resolves to chord tone F on B♭Maj7, which lasts for seven beats.

Additional counterpoint can be added in third and fourth voices with the two remaining basic chord tones.

They may move in *parallel* motion (the same direction by the same interval), *contrary* motion (the opposite direction), *oblique* motion (one voice doesn't move, the other does), or *similar* motion (the same direction by a different interval).

TRACK 53

Fig. 17.3. Four-Part Counterpoint

  c. If you skip a note in your counterpoint, return in the opposite direction by step.

TRACK 54

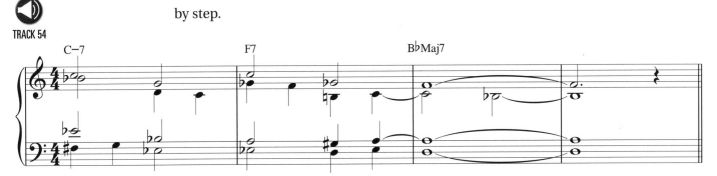

Fig. 17.4. Skips and Suspensions

d. Use suspensions where possible.

e. When your melody is active, use sustaining notes in the counterpoint.

Fig. 17.5. Rhythmically Active Melody and Final Resolution

PRACTICE

Exercise 17.1. Four-Part Counterpoint

Play and analyze the following four-part counterpoint.

Exercise 17.2. Writing Two-Part Counterpoint

Arrange counterpoint to the melodies from the lead sheets in appendix A using the harmony provided.

Exercise 17.3. Writing Three- and Four-Part Counterpoint

Add a third and fourth voice to the counterpoint you wrote for exercise 17.2. Remember to choose your notes based on the chord tones missing from the first two lines.

CHAPTER 18

Additional Harmonizations

Harmonic supply may be increased by working backwards between original terminal points—the basic chords of the tune that the composer intended. Using the melody as a controller, take V7 of the chord being approached or its substitute dominant. The melody note must be a chord tone or tension.

Fig. 18.1. "Theme for John" Harmonized with Dominant 7 Chords

SUBSTITUTE DOMINANT 7 CHORDS

If you have a dominant 7 chord approaching its tonic chord, you can reharmonize that dominant 7 chord with a *substitute dominant 7 chord*. A substitute dominant 7 chord (subV7) is a dominant chord with a root a ♭5 interval from the root of the original dominant 7 chord. Both contain the same tritone.

For example, in the key of C, the dominant 7 chord is G7, and the substitute dominant 7 chord of G7 is D♭7. The tritone of B/C♭ and F occurs in both.

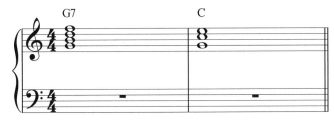

Fig. 18.2. V7 to I in C Major

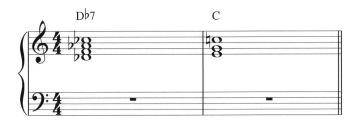

Fig. 18.3. SubV7 to I in C Major

REPLACING DOMINANT 7 CHORDS WITH MINOR 7 CHORDS

You may convert any dominant 7th into a sus4 chord, which in turn becomes a minor 7th chord. D7sus4 becomes A–7. F7 becomes C–7. Any dominant 7 can be preceded by its own related II–7 chord. Any minor 7 can be preceded by its related V7.

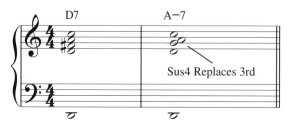

Fig. 18.4. Sus4 Replaces the 3rd

SPECIAL VOICINGS

Try these special voicings, either for harmonizing a melody or for left-hand support. For borderline assessments, use your ear.

Chord	Special Voicing
Dominant 7 chord with any notes in the symmetric diminished scale	1, 5, 3, ♭9
Nondiatonic dominant 7th chords II7, ♭II7, ♭III7, IV7, ♭VI7, ♭VII7	♮9, ♮13, 3, 7 -or- ♭5, ♮13, 3, 7 -or- ♭5, ♮13, 3, 7
Dominant 7 chord with ♭5 in the melody	♭5, 3, 1, ♭7
Minor 7 or Minor 7♭5 chords with 11 in the melody	11, ♭3, 1, ♭7

Here's an example of 1-5-3-♭9 voicing used with melody notes found in the symmetrical diminished scale.

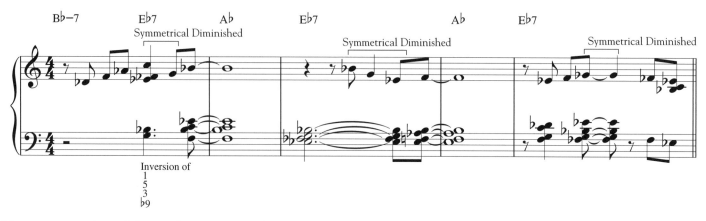

Fig. 18.5. 1-5-3-♭9 Voicing with Symmetrical Diminished Scale in "Perry's Parasol"

PRACTICE

Practice this exercise to see how dominant 7th chords can be used to create forward motion in a progression.

Exercise 18.1. Directional Configuration of Dominant Structures

The two rows of chord symbols below are interchangeable; you can build a progression using any combination from either row.

The bottom row of chord symbols shows the original V7 of V relationships. The top row is the substitute dominants, a diminished above the roots of the originals. Both must contain the same tritone, which is why they are interchangeable. The third and root of the chord are stable. The seventh adds instability and requires resolution.

The original dominant may be preceded by its original V7 or by its substitute dominant. This results in descending chromatic root motion.

Practice this in every key choosing different cadential points from each line (as shown in bar 1).

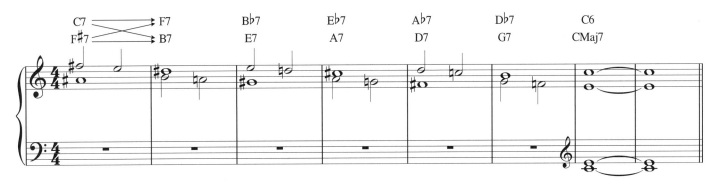

Exercise 18.2. Related II–7

Any dominant 7th may be preceded by its related II–7 or the related II–7 of its substitute dominant. Find the tonic of the dominant and take the II–7 in that key. Again, the two lines of chords are interchangeable. For example, in the first measure, the D–7 is the related II–7 of the original V7 of C–7, which is G7. Therefore, the D–7 can go to Db7 to C–7, resulting in chromatic root motion.

Exercise 18.2 shows two systems. The bottom system draws from possibilities in the top system.

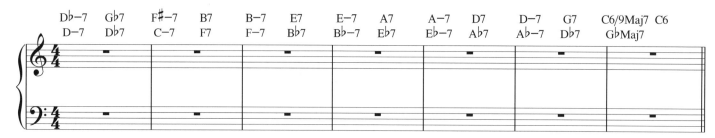

Practice this by finding terminal points in the lead sheets in appendix A, and trying these different possibilities, using the melody as a controller. For example, try measures 22–23 of "Like, Blues." In bar 23, the terminal point is F7, with B♮ in the melody. Take V7 of F7 (C7), then find the substitute dominant of that (G♭7). The G♭7 moves nicely to F7.

Exercise 18.3. Combining V of V, V of II, Substitute Dominants, and Their Related II–7ths

The bottom system shows a melody that is used as a controller for the above progression. Choose your own chords to apply these relationships to the given lead line.

APPENDIX A

Lead Sheets

The following lead sheets are performed in two ways on the CD: arranged for solo piano (fully notated in appendix B) and for jazz combo. The CD features recordings of each, plus play-along tracks (without piano), for your practice.

Lead sheets are a common way to communicate musical ideas, particularly in jazz. Notice that our band took liberties with many aspects of the written charts: melody, rhythm, harmony, groove, and form. Similarly, I encourage you to create your own unique interpretations when working from lead sheets.

This chart shows some of the techniques you should try when you practice playing from these lead sheets.

Piece	Technique to Apply	Measures
"Theme for John"	V7 of V	5, 11
	SubV	5, 11
	Increase chord supply using V7 or subV7 with selected melody notes	6
	Diminished approach	9
	5-Part diatonic voicings in fourths	10
	Use 6/9 chords in L.H.	19
	1-5-3-♭9 inversion	19
	Triadic harmonization with variable bass	19, 20
"Perry's Parasol"	SubV7 where possible (voice with upper-structure triads)	1, 2
	Voice with upper structure triads and upper-structure fourths	1, 3
	Voice using upper-structure triads	2, 3
	Apply consecutive fingers and add coupling notes	16–17
	Apply 1-5-3-♭9 voicing in left hand and subV	17
"Take Two"	A♭7 IV7 (No 1-5-3-♭9)	2
	A♭7 subV of D7 (No 1-5-3-♭9)	4, 12, 13
	Use 1-5-3-♭9 voicing	11
"Like, Blues"	SubV on 2nd E♭	1
	SubV on note C to F7	6
	SubVs	6, 8
	SubVs	8, 24
	SubVs (1-5-3-♭9)	30,32
"Sapphire"	Diatonic and non-diatonic triads/variable bass	19, 20, 21
	Diatonic and non-diatonic triads with variable bass	30
	Use 1-5-3-♭9 voicing, subV, and II–7	32

Like, Blues

TRACK 2   TRACK 3
(Trio)   (Play Along)

Ray Santisi

Theme for John

TRACK 5
(Trio)

TRACK 6
(Play Along)

Ray Santisi

Perry's Parasol

TRACK 8
(Trio)

TRACK 9
(Play Along)

Ray Santisi

Take Two

TRACK 11
(Trio)

TRACK 12
(Play Along)

Ray Santisi

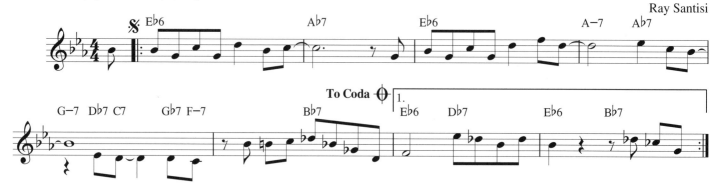

Sapphire

TRACK 14
(Trio)

TRACK 15
(Play Along)

Ray Santisi

APPENDIX B

Etudes

The following etudes are solo-piano arrangements of the lead sheets presented in appendix A. They illustrate many techniques presented in this book's lessons.

It is relatively rare for jazz to be notated in such precision, but useful for pedagogical purposes.

Like, Blues

TRACK 1

Ray Santisi

Theme for John

TRACK 4

Ray Santisi

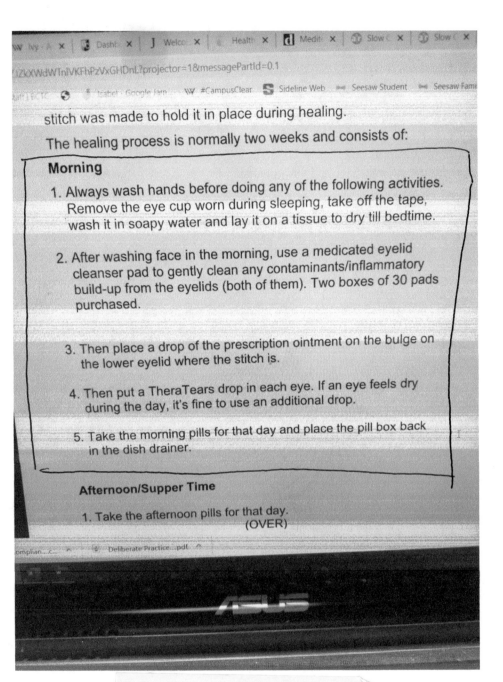

W Ivy - A × | Dashb × | J Welco × | Health × | Medit × | Slow C × | Slow C ×

...ZtXWdWTnlVKFhPzVxGHDnL?projector=1&messagePartId=0.1

Isabel - Google Jam   W #CampusClear   S Sideline Web   Seesaw Student   Seesaw Fami

stitch was made to hold it in place during healing.

The healing process is normally two weeks and consists of:

Morning

1. Always wash hands before doing any of the following activities. Remove the eye cup worn during sleeping, take off the tape, wash it in soapy water and lay it on a tissue to dry till bedtime.

2. After washing face in the morning, use a medicated eyelid cleanser pad to gently clean any contaminants/inflammatory build-up from the eyelids (both of them). Two boxes of 30 pads purchased.

3. Then place a drop of the prescription ointment on the bulge on the lower eyelid where the stitch is.

4. Then put a TheraTears drop in each eye. If an eye feels dry during the day, it's fine to use an additional drop.

5. Take the morning pills for that day and place the pill box back in the dish drainer.

Afternoon/Supper Time

1. Take the afternoon pills for that day.
(OVER)

omplian...c...   Deliberate Practice...pdf

For Mark
Singer
leave in Room

Perry's Parasol

TRACK 7

Ray Santisi

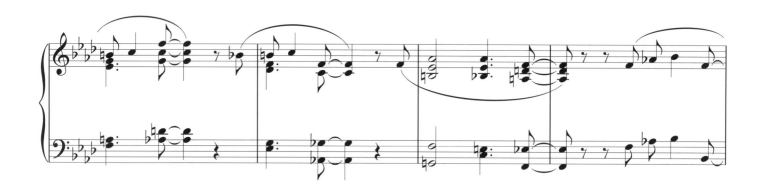

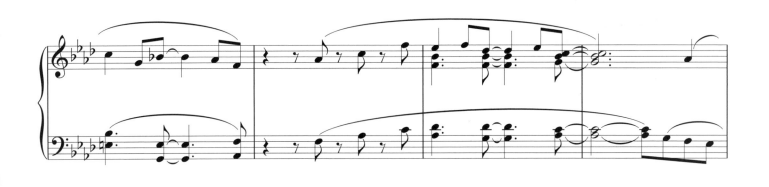

Take Two

TRACK 10

Ray Santisi

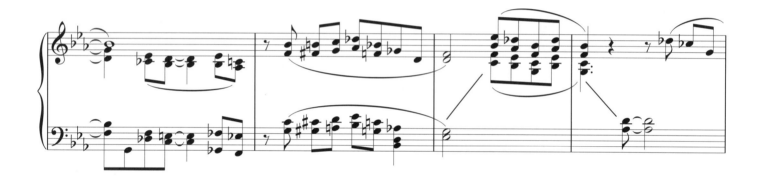

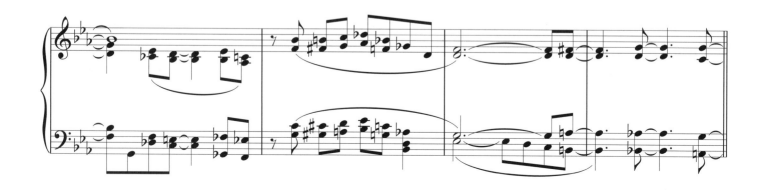

Sapphire

TRACK 13

Ray Santisi

Berklee College of Music Piano Requirements

The following list outlines the minimum departmental requirements of all piano majors at Berklee College of Music, current as of 2009. All these topics, among many others, are discussed in this book.

Level 1. Chords voice-led left hand with 7th chords; melody and/or improvisation right hand.

Level 2. Chords voice-led with tensions left hand; melody and/or improvisation right hand.

Level 3. Chords voice-led left hand demonstrating continued use of tensions; melody with coupling notes right hand *or* melody harmonized right hand, bass activity left hand.

Level 4. Basic open voicing techniques for harmonizing melody (examples of suggested voicings available on Piano Department Web site).

Level 5. Continued open-voicing techniques (including upper-structure triads) for harmonizing melody; transposition of tunes to two other keys in addition to the original *or* an arrangement involving a minimum of three keys.

Level 6. Voicings in fourths for harmonization of melody; continued transposition to more difficult keys. Use of keys as described in level 5.

Lee Silverman Voice Treatment
To regain communication and active living

The Lee Silverman Voice Treatment, LSVT®, is a proven effective treatment program that restores physical activity and oral communication in individuals with Parkinson Disease.

Patients, family members, and professionals observe that patients are more effective and emotionally engaged communicators and as well as being more active. Patients are able to participate fully and improve the quality of their life after LSVT®.

Who can benefit from LSVT BIG® and LSVT LOUD® ? Individuals with:

- Multiple sclerosis
- Stroke
- Aging voice
- Vocal fold paralysis.
- Parkinson's Disease
- Cerebral Palsy
- Ataxic Dysarthria from CVA or TBI
- Down Syndrome

What is involved in the treatment?

- Intense: 4 sessions per week for one month
- Sessions are 1 hour long
- Individualized for each patient
- Functional movement or speaking tasks and daily homework

How can LSVT BIG® and LSVT LOUD® help?

LSVT Loud® and LSVT BIG® specifically targets the phonatory and motor system in a systematic, functional treatment process by a certified clinician.

- Improves vocal loudness, intonation, and voice quality
- Addresses common problems of disordered articulation, diminished facial expression, and impaired swallowing
- Targets unique movement impairments
- Improves speed, balance and quality of life
- Increases trunk rotation and gait

Individualized care plan

Rehab specialists skilled in a vast range of programming

Rehab services covered under most insurance companies

Helping patients return to a more independent functional lifestyle

Excellent customer service

Glossary

6/9 chord: major 6 chord with tension 9 substituting the root

activated modal framework: a series of harmonies where chord tones are connected by material taken from the mode

altered dominant approach chord: dominant-7th chord with altered tensions of its target chord

anticipation: syncopated rhythm that occurs before the original attack

approach note: points of tension that require resolution to a target note

broken chord: chord tones played sequentially rather than simultaneously

carrier chord: broken chords with tensions that move to a target note (3rd [strongest], root, or 5th)

chord tones: notes in their associated chord symbol

chromatic approach chord: approach chord based on a root a half step away from any chord tone (or tension) of its target chord

close position: voicing in which all notes are set within an octave

comping: chordal part that accompanies a melody

consonance: major third, minor third, perfect fifth, major sixth, minor sixth, octave

contrary motion: moving the opposite direction

counterpoint: one note played against another; both are harmonically complementary

coupling note: a chord tone or tension used to harmonize a melody note, creating chord fragments

delay: syncopated rhythm that occurs after the original attack

delayed resolution: a technique of playing neighbor tones before resolving to a chord tone

derivative bass line: a bass line that contains notes other than the roots of chords

diatonic fourth voicing: fourth voicing that includes notes from a scale associated with its key

diminished approach chord: diminished chord based on a root a half step below the target chord root

dissonance: minor second and major seventh (sharp dissonance), major second and minor seventh (mild dissonance)

drop-2 voicing: an open voicing built from a basic 4-part close voicing by dropping the voice that is second from the top down an octave

drop-2 and -4 voicing: an open voicing built from a basic 4-part close voicing by dropping the voices that are second and fourth from the top down an octave

drop-3 voicing: an open voicing built from a basic 4-part close voicing by dropping the third voice from the top down an octave

drop-4 voicing: an open voicing built from a 4-part close voicing by dropping the fourth voice from the top down an octave and adding the root

first inversion: voicing in which the 3rd is on the bottom

fourth voicing: open voicings built with fourth intervals

guide tones: the 3rd and 7th degrees of a chord

harmonizing: reinforcing a melody with chords

intervallic links: a contemporary improvisation practice in which intervals (excluding tritones) are linked using whole or half steps

inversion: note order, defined by the voicing's bottom note

key center: harmonic region preceded by cadential material

lead line: the melody of a tune

melodizing: playing broken chords in the right hand

mode: a scale that contains a characteristic pitch that distinguishes it from the major or minor scale from which it is derived

non-chord tones: dissonances; notes not in its associated chord

non-diatonic fourth voicing: fourth voicing built with perfect fourth intervals

oblique motion: in counterpoint, a situation in which one voice moves while the other does not

open voicing: a chord that is spread larger than an octave

parallel approach chord: approach chord in which all the voices move the same interval to the target

parallel motion: moving the same direction by the same interval

particalized random comping: a type of random comping in which parts of a chord are played rather than an entire voicing

pentatonic scale: five-note scale derived from the major scale

permutation: possible way that intervals may be related

pianisticize: using methods that broaden playing away from standard pedantic techniques

random comping: playing voicings that aren't necessarily voice led, using syncopation

rhythmic displacement: an improvisation technique in which a motif is played by a rhythmic unit earlier or later

root position: voicing in which chord root is on the bottom

second inversion: voicing in which the 5th is on the bottom

similar motion: moving the same direction by a different interval

stepwise diatonic approach chord: approach chord that belongs to the key of the progression and harmonizes a melody moving by step

subdivision: rhythmic unit within a beat

substitute dominant 7 chord: a dominant chord with a root a ♭5 interval from the root of the original dominant 7 chord

suspension: harmony where the 3rd is replaced with the 4th

symmetric diminished scale: scale comprised of alternating half and whole steps

syncopating: playing a rhythm on an offbeat

target note: chord tone on a strong beat; a landing point

tension: a note that extends a basic chord, such as 9, 11, or 13

tension resolution: aspect of jazz counterpoint in which tensions on chords must resolve to certain scale degrees

tension substitution: replacing chord tones with tensions for greater harmonic interest

terminal points: the basic chords of the tune that the composer intended

third inversion: voicing in which the 6th or 7th is on the bottom

tritone: 3rd and 7th of any dominant

upper-structure fourth voicing: three notes built in perfect fourths, with (from the top) the 9, ♯9, and 3 or ♭13, 13, ♭7

upper-structure triad: a triad that contains one or more tensions

voice leading: choosing inversions that minimize note movement

walking bass line: bass line in which a note is played on every beat, usually with an implied triplet feel

window: space in music, provided by a sustained melody note, that allows for improvisational material

About the Author

Ray Santisi has been a professor of piano at Berklee College of Music since 1957.

He has taught thousands of students, including Diana Krall, Makoto Ozone, Joe Zawinul, Keith Jarrett, and Jane Ira Bloom.

An internationally known jazz pianist, Santisi has performed alongside legends Charlie Parker, Stan Getz, Mel Torme, Irene Kral, Natalie Cole, and others, and appeared on many major-label recordings. He recently received a nomination as a 2008 inductee to the IAJE Jazz Education Hall of Fame. Among other honors, he has received grants and awards from the National Endowment for the Arts for both performance and composition.

He currently plays in a variety of jazz venues with his New England-based piano trio, the Real Thing.